Dick King-Smith

JUNGLE JINGLES

and Other Animal Poems

Illustrations by
Jonathan Allen

DOUBLEDAY

London · New York · Toronto · Sydney · Auckland

TRANSWORLD PUBLISHERS LTD
61-63 Uxbridge Road, London W5 5SA

TRANSWORLD PUBLISHERS (AUSTRALIA) PTY LTD
15-23 Helles Avenue, Moorebank, NSW 2170

TRANSWORLD PUBLISHERS (NZ) LTD
Cnr Moselle and Waipareira Aves,
Henderson, Auckland

DOUBLEDAY CANADA LTD
105 Bond Street, Toronto, Ontario M5B 1Y3

Published 1990 by Doubleday
a division of Transworld Publishers Ltd

Copyright © 1990 by Dick King-Smith
Illustrations copyright © 1990 by Jonathan Allen

British Library Cataloguing in Publication Data
King-Smith, Dick
Jungle jingles and other animal poems.
I. Title   II. Allen, Jonathan, 1957-
821.914

ISBN 0–385–40109–4

Printed in Great Britain by
BPCC Paulton Books Limited

Contents

JUNGLE JINGLES

AND OTHER ANIMAL POEMS

Jungle Jingles

The jungle is a fearful place
To members of the human race
Who happen to be passing through
And are not sure of what to do
In jungles, and with baited breath
Are full of thoughts of sudden death
Beneath the paws and jaws and claws
Of terrifying carnivores.

Fear not. The jungle, you should know,
Can be a thrilling place to go
Provided that you do not sin
Against the beasts that live therein.
Shoot them with camera, not gun,
Respect them, each and every one,
And never take them unawares –
The jungle isn't yours, it's theirs.

However, should you find some day –
In spite of everything I say –
That jungles fill you with alarm,
A useful way of staying calm
And keeping cool and passing time
Is to recite a little rhyme,
You'll find your fear will soon have gone.
So here are one or two. Read on.

?!

Should you meet a herd of Zebras,
And you cannot tell the hebras
Of the Zebras from the shebras –
Watch which way each Zebra peebras.

No Wings, No Tail, Two Names

The Kiwi's a bird with another appellation –
The Apteryx. And, should you ever chance to mention
This spellbinding fact to a friend or a relation,
It's apteryxcite their immediate attention.

In the Soup

A wagging tail will tell you that
A Dog is overjoyed;
In contradiction to a Cat,
Which wags when it's annoyed.

The Ox's tail, one has to state,
Seems mournfully to droop:
It's just as though it knew its fate –
To end as oxtail soup.

Tit for Tat

The Anteater has always fed
On Ants, but when at last he's dead,
The Ants will feed on him instead.

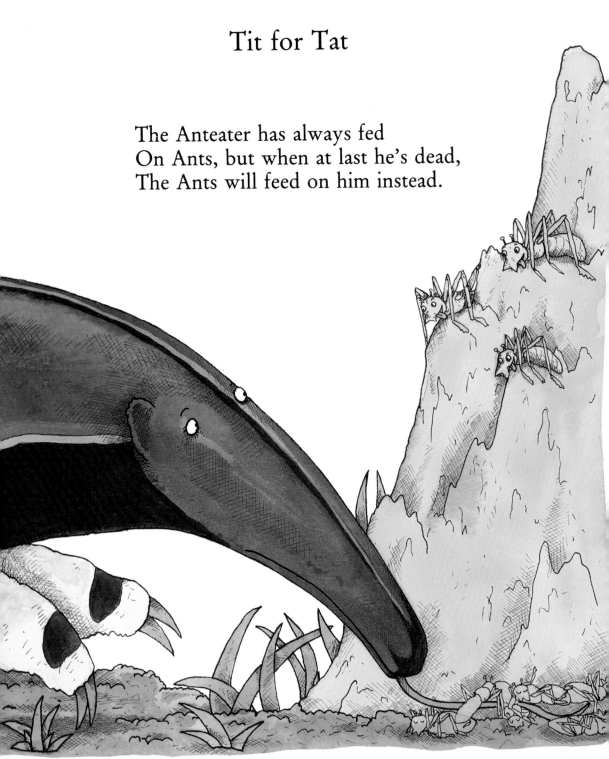

Strippers

If you fall in a river that's full of Piranha,
They'll strip off your flesh like you'd skin a banana.
There's no time for screaming, there's no time for groans.
In forty-five seconds you're nothing but bones.

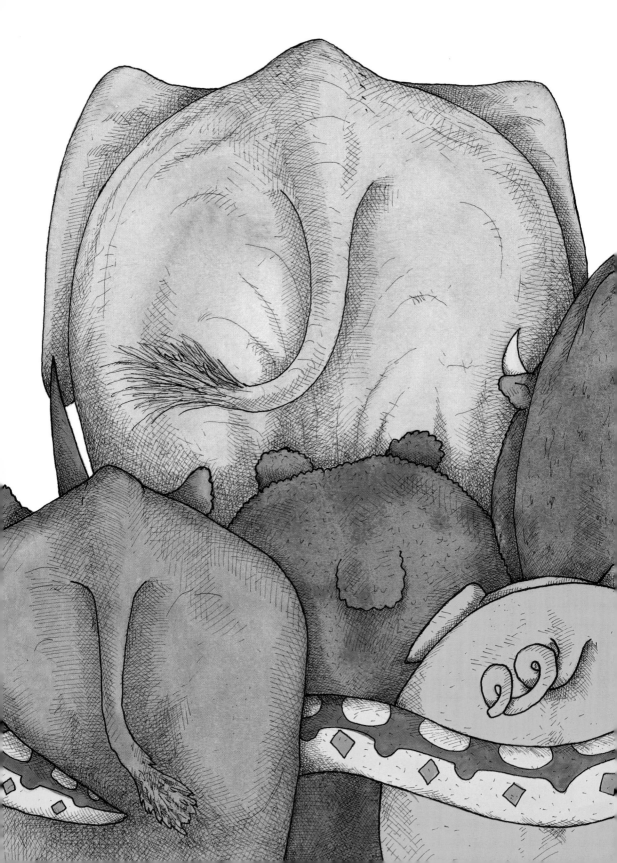

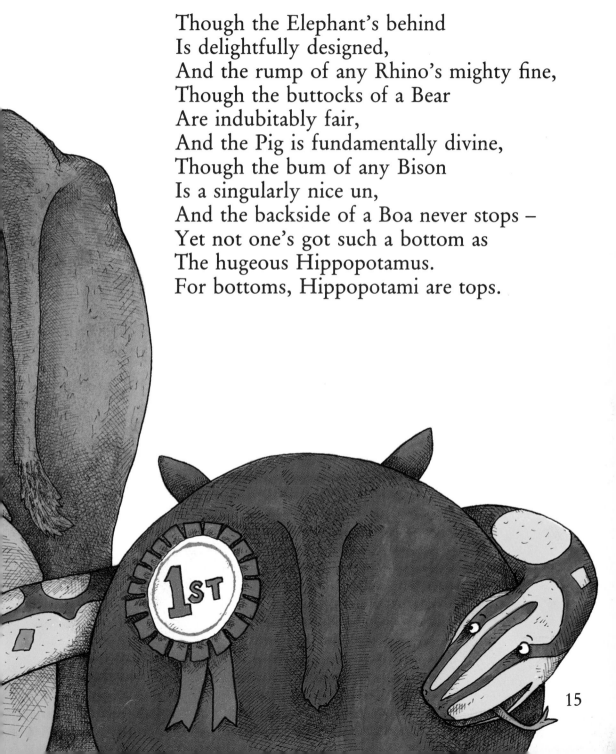

Look Back in Wonder

Though the Elephant's behind
Is delightfully designed,
And the rump of any Rhino's mighty fine,
Though the buttocks of a Bear
Are indubitably fair,
And the Pig is fundamentally divine,
Though the bum of any Bison
Is a singularly nice un,
And the backside of a Boa never stops –
Yet not one's got such a bottom as
The hugeous Hippopotamus.
For bottoms, Hippopotami are tops.

Enough to Make You Sick

What if every day you ate
Food of twice your body-weight?
That is what the Pygmy Shrew
(Just to stay alive) must do.
Think what it would mean to you.

Seven bucketfuls of chips,
Several dozen Instant Whips,
Twenty packs of Shredded Wheat,
Thirty tins of luncheon meat –
That is what you'd have to eat.

Plus – six chickens and a ham,
Forty-seven pots of jam,
Fifty bars of Milky Way.
All that in a single day!
'Lovely!' did I hear you say?

Thank your lucky stars that you
Were not born a Pygmy Shrew.

17

Splat!

No creature can create it
Or hope to imitate it.
To do this thing no other beast knows how.

However much they practise,
The plain and simple fact is –
No-one can make a cowpat like a Cow.

Lost for Words

A little whistling note to call its calf.
That is the only noise the tall Giraffe
Can make. Apart from that, it has no choice
But silence, for it doesn't have a voice.
For joy the tall Giraffe can never shout –
Its mouth will open, but no sound comes out.
And if it's sad or wounded or bereaved,
What happens must be seen to be believed,
For silently, out of each liquid eye,
The tears come dropping from the very sky.
Be kindly then, and never never laugh
At that dumb animal, the tall Giraffe.

Suck it and See

The taste of blood, observers note,
Is most appealing to the Stoat,
Which grabs a rabbit by the throat,
And dines upon it, table-d'hôte.

His and Hers

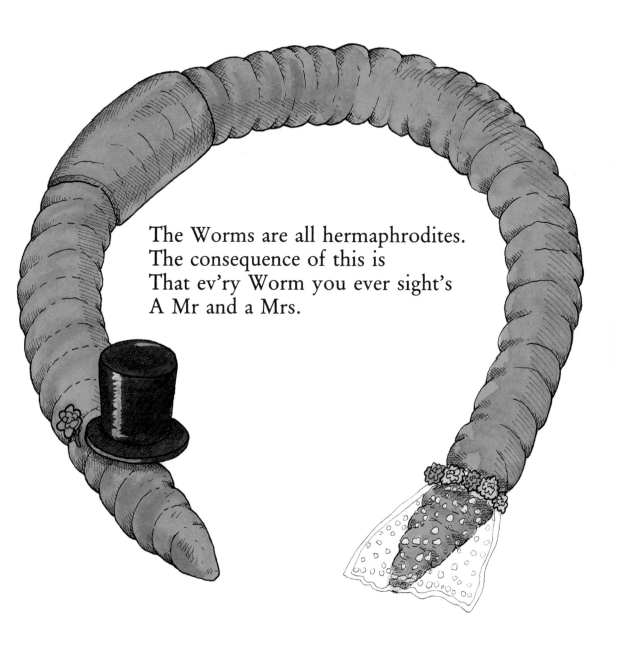

The Worms are all hermaphrodites.
The consequence of this is
That ev'ry Worm you ever sight's
A Mr and a Mrs.

Take Cover

The Vulture feeds on the deceased
Of absolutely ev'ry beast.
It isn't fussy in the least
And any body makes a feast.

All corpses serve to appetize
And none escapes the Vulture's eyes.
As soon as any creature dies,
Down drops the Vulture from the skies.

Remember then – before you're dead –
It's better if you die in bed
Or even in the garden shed
If there are Vultures overhead.

We Have Lift-Off

Young Gannets like practising flying
In their nests on the high narrow ledges.
The impetuous things
Keep on flapping their wings
While perched on the ultimate edges.

But all of the time that they're trying,
They are fearful of premature motion.
So they're careful to stand
Facing in towards land
And keeping their backs to the ocean.

Best Foot Forward

You thought the Centipede possessed
Exactly fifty pairs of feet?
Is that the figure you'd have guessed?
The answer isn't quite so neat.

For scientific men who've seen
Each centipedal cousin,
Find some have only got fifteen
And some have fifteen dozen.

Catcall

The Puma (or the Mountain Lion
Or Cougar or the Catamount)
May have no need of that amount
Of labels to rely on.

But when he fancies lambs to eat
All farmers curse him till they're hoarse.
They call the Puma names too coarse
And vulgar to repeat.

Seaside Suicide

When Lemmings migrate, and arrive at a river,
They plummet right in it with never a shiver
And swim till their feet touch the ground.

When Lemmings migrate, and arrive at a lake,
They swim straight across it, and out with a shake,
And onward relentlessly bound.

And then, when the Lemmings' migratory host
Has crossed the whole land and arrived at the coast,
They swim out to sea and are drowned.

Like It or Lump It

The Camel sports a brace of humps,
The Dromedary only one.
It looks as though it's in the dumps
And never having any fun.
The reason, so the experts tell us,
Is that the Dromedary's jealous.

A Family Picnic

If you meet with a man-eating Tiger,
Don't think that it only eats men.
When it's polished off Dad, it'll start on your mother,
Your sister, your auntie, your new baby brother,
And shortly be hungry again.

For afters, it might manage you and your gran,
So don't think a man-eater only eats man.

Tale of a Tail

The Boodie is a quarter-size
Relation of the Kangaroo.
You hardly would believe your eyes
When witnessing what Boodies do
To make their nests. Each picks up straw
And puts it on its hairy tail
Which curls around, to squeeze it more
And more, and make a little bale.

Salute the Boodie, tail compactly curled!
First-ever pick-up baler in the world!

Fore and Aft

The Mole, which tunnels very well,
Can find its way by touch and smell:
The many bristles on its nose
Send messages as down it goes.
And though it's practically blind,
It has a sensitive behind –
Just one of Nature's many mercies
And useful when the Mole reverses.

Horse Sense

The Suffolk Punch eats grass for lunch
In spring and summer – that's to say,
In winter it is fed on hay.
There is a difference of course
From any lesser breed of horse –
The Suffolk Punch eats twice as munch.

Free Ride

When the babies of the Crocodile
Hatch out beside the River Nile,
And first emerge upon its sandy shores,
She transports her sons and daughters
To the safety of its waters,
Holding all of them within her mighty jaws.
See how tenderly she holds her little crew!
(But I shouldn't let her try it on with you.)

Hear! Hear!

Though you may feel a little fear
If there's an Earwig in your ear,
There is no cause for utter dread –
It can't get right inside your head.
But on the whole it might be best
To shift the creature, lest it nest.
An ear that's used for Earwig-rearing
Could cause you partial loss of hearing.

Gulp!

The Pike has one abiding wish –
To swallow any other fish.
It isn't fussy, doesn't mind
What sort, but gobbles any kind.
In fact, it's guaranteed to like
The chance to eat another Pike.

Phew!

There's nothing on earth that's ever stunk
As bad as a squirt from an angry Skunk.
There's nothing as foul and nothing as strong –
A squirt from a Skunk is the world's worst pong.

You must leave your house, and you can't return
Till they've fumigated it, while you burn
The furnishings and your clothes as well.
You stand there naked and still you smell.

I'll give you a tip (and this is true):
If an angry Skunk ever squirts on you,
The only thing that's of any use
Is a long cold bath in tomato juice.

Fishing Finger

The Aye-Aye has a finger that's meticulously planned.
It's quite unlike the other fingers on the Aye-Aye's hand.
It's long and strong and bony and it's very very thin,
And when he finds a beetle's hole, the Aye-Aye sticks it in,
Unbends it and extends it and then wiggles it about,
And pulls a lot of lovely squashy beetle-larvae out.
Which only goes to demonstrate what any Aye-Aye knew –
That all these little lemurs have a very high I.Q.

A Game of Squash

If there's one thing that's worse than a Headlouse,
Then it must, I suppose, be a Bedlouse.
But as I've understood lice
(And excepting the Woodlice),
Why, the only good louse is a dead louse.

Jolly Blue Giant

The Blue's the biggest kind of Whale
At thirty metres, top to tail.
The largest creature on the earth
(It's seven metres long at birth!)
And as for weight, it's twenty-five
Times any elephant alive.
If you should meet one face to face,
You need not swim away apace
In fear, or even show alarm,
The Blue won't do you any harm.
It isn't that Blue Whales are wimps.
It's just that all they eat is shrimps.

Starting from Scratch

Have you ever been bird-spotting
And observed a Starling squatting
On an ants' nest, and you wonder
As you watch it, why in thunder
Is the silly creature doing
Something it must soon be rueing?
I'll explain.

Parasites that drive it frantic
Make the bird perform this antic,
Knowing ants will then infest it
And efficiently divest it
Of the pests, with formic acid,
Rendering the Starling placid
Once again.

Down the Hatch

The Python can unlock its jaws
To gape as wide as double doors,
And then the snake expands its throat
And swallows whole a nanny-goat
Or pig or antelope or sheep,
And goes contentedly to sleep,
Its middle one enormous bulge,
The shape of which does not divulge
What wretched animal has died.
Let's hope it's never you inside
The Python. If it were, my friend,
That, without doubt, would be

THE END

47